For my littles. Mommy loves you very much.
All praises to the Most High for His vision and provision.

• • • • • • • • • • • • • • • •

This book is based on the events found in Exodus (שמות) chapters 3 through 12

This Passover Book belongs to:

_____

From a blazing bush, Yahuah spoke to Moses.

"I AM WHO I AM.

Go and tell Pharaoh to let my people go, and I will be with you."

Pharaoh, the king of Egypt, had been cruel to the Israelites. Yahuah heard the Israelites crying out to Him. This is why He chose Moses to speak to Pharaoh.

But Moses was terrified to speak to Pharaoh.

So Yahuah said that his brother, Aaron, could speak for him.

Moses and Aaron went to Pharaoh and said, "Let my people go."

Pharaoh said, "No!"

Yahuah told Moses that because Pharaoh's heart is hardened, He is going to send plagues to Egypt.

First, Moses used his staff to strike the water in the Nile River. The water turned into blood (דם)! All the fish died. That water smelled horrible and was undrinkable!

But Pharaoh did not let Yahuah's people go.

Next, Aaron stretched out his staff over the water, and frogs (צפרדעים) emerged. They were hopping everywhere!

Pharaoh said, "You can go tomorrow."

But Pharaoh did not let Yahuah's people go.

Then Yahuah sent a plague of lice. Aaron struck the dust with his staff and all the dust turned to lice (כינים). The lice crawled all over the Egyptians and their animals.

But Pharaoh did not let Yahuah's people go.

Moses told Pharaoh, "Yahuah says to let my people go."

Pharaoh said, "No!"

After that, Yahuah sent swarms (ערב) of flies. They covered everything!

But no flies were in Goshen, where the Israelites lived.

Then, Pharaoh said, "You can worship here."

Moses said, "No, we must go."

Pharaoh said, "OK. You can go."

But Pharaoh did not let Yahuah's people go.

Then, Yahuah sent a plague (דבר) upon the animals in Egypt and caused them to get sick.

But the animals in Goshen were alive and well.

Still Pharaoh did not let Yahuah's people go.

After that, Yahuah infected the Egyptians' skin.

They were covered with boils (שחין)!

But the Israelites did not get sick at all.

And Pharaoh still did not let Yahuah's people go.

Then, Yahuah hurled hail (ברד) and fire from the sky!

Pharaoh said, "Okay, okay! I will let you go."

After he let the people go, Pharaoh changed his mind and made them come back.

Moses and Aaron told Pharaoh, "If you will not let Yahuah's people go, He will send locusts (ארבה) to devour your crops."

Pharaoh said, "Only the men can go. No one else!"

After that, Yahuah sent a plague of locusts.

There were so many locusts that the sky was full of them and they ate all of the Egyptian's crops!

Then there was complete darkness (חושך), but only in Egypt.

"I can't see!" the people said.

But there was light in Goshen, where the Israelites lived.

And Pharaoh said, "Your whole family can go, but leave your animals."

Moses said, "We need our animals to go with us." But because Pharaoh's heart was as hard as a rock, he would not let Yahuah's people go.

Then Moses told the Israelites to slaughter a lamb and to wipe the blood onto their doorposts.

"Yahuah will go through the land and strike down all the firstborn. Yet, when He sees the blood on the doorposts of the Israelites, He will pass over those houses."

This is why it is called Passover (פסח).

Then Yahuah told Moses, "This month shall be the first month of the year for you. Remember and keep this feast day, throughout your generations, forever. You shall also celebrate the Feast of Unleavened Bread. Take all of the leaven out of your houses and eat unleavened bread for seven days. You shall celebrate this day, throughout your generations, forever."

Moses and Aaron told Pharaoh what Yahuah said that He would do.

But Pharaoh did not listen.

That night, Yahuah struck down the firstborn (בכור) of every household that did not have the blood of the lamb on their doorpost.

The Egyptians were very sad,
and all of their families cried.

Finally, Pharaoh said, "I will let Yahuah's people go." And he did.

And the Israelites were free to go to the Promised Land to worship Yahuah.

Hebrew Vocabulary

Exodus	שמות	(Shemot)
blood	דם	(dam)
frogs	צפרדעים	(ṣ-p̄ar-də-ʾîm)
lice	כינים	(kin-nām)
swarms	ערב	(ʾā-rōḇ)
plague	דבר	(de·ḇer)
boils	שחין	(šə-ḥîn;)
hail	ברד	(bā-rāḏ)
locusts	ארבה	(ʾar-beh)
darkness	חושך	(ḥo-shek)
Passover	פסח	(pe-saḥ)
firstborn	בכור	(bə-ḵō-wr)

*Hebrew words are read from right to left.

CPSIA information can be obtained
at www.ICGtesting.com
Printed in the USA
BVHW011428140422
634332BV00014B/525